Baby, Boom, Boom—
Baby, It's You!

Baby, Boom, Boom— Baby, It's You!

Terry Wayne Brownlee

Library of Congress Control Number: 2010917831
ISBN: Hardcover   978-1-4568-2492-1
                Softcover   978-1-4568-2491-4
                Ebook   978-1-4568-2493-8

To order additional copies of this book, contact:
Xlibris Corporation
1-888-795-4274
www.Xlibris.com
Orders@Xlibris.com
86729

CONTENTS

Dedicated to:

Ms M. Penny, for pointing out my special qualities. To all my loving, crazy, silly friends, who always pushed me to go further. My teachers, and to myself, for never accepting no, as an answer.

INTRODUCTION

Hey, big spender, yeah, you with the big greenbacks. You used to be big, now, nothing but big debts. What happened, Bill? Hey, big spender! Where are you now? We all started out the same in the 1950s. We sat in front of the TV day after day with our family, getting more sucked into hearing the same jingle into our heads to buy their products. We were a part of the TV golden age. So many good shows—*I Love Lucy*; *Have Gun, Will Travel*; and the family favorite every Sunday, *The Ed Sullivan Show*. Then there were all the great movies we saw—*The Three Stooges*, *The Bowery Boys*, *Tarzan*, and so many British comedies and monster movies. Many that would inspire future filmmakers such a Steven Spielberg to make dazzling films in the 1979. Little did we know, many of the movies we were watching were the same films our own parents grew up with, only they had radio and all the classic shows that held them spellbound, all heavily sponsored and making sure kids ate the right cereal and we drank the right coffee. So it began—the persuasive power of advertising and how it begins to manipulate into the consumer we were so to become. Its roots go much farther back, back as far back as the seventeenth century. A movement of the age of advertising had begun. Pioneers such as Adam Smith (1773-90) with the image of an invisible hand held to inaugurate a powerful, almost mystical belief in the marketplace as the guiding institution for a modernizing society. "Smith saw in the market force for economic rationality a force that could shape and spire the pattern of social development independent of the begins of the eighteenth century Europe." How could I persuade you into wanting to understand how marketing strategy worked on children's programming and the popular culture market (more to follow as we explore each decade)?

It began for me one stormy night when I was born, June 18, 1946, on a Wednesday; they say a Wednesday child is full of woe. I was also part of the baby boom generation; we were to be the largest demographic in history, different for the following reasons: Our parents were survivors of the Great Depression and World War II. They were determined that their children would be better and never be without. "After the War, we would be living in a time of affluence. We would be more educated, healthier, more influence sophisticated."

Television and movies introduced us kids to marketing strategy, giving us heroes and villains, rock and roll, and movie stars that shaped each decade. What would you like to be when you grow up—a cowboy, secret agent, scuba diver, spaceman, or flying nun? All in our living room for us to dream and hope we could be exactly like that, all setting up to spend. Where was I, were you. And most important is how we spent our money as each decade ended and new challenges for advertisers to reinvent themselves, and as the times and technology changed, so too more products to buy. Fortunes would be made with such products as Magic Marker, Silly Putty, and Monopoly. By 1959, another product came out that touched lives of little girls everywhere; her name was Barbie. She became the biggest seller of all time. "The Campaign revealed that toy makers could borrow from establish media and redesign them for their own purpose, retaining control over identity profile and position." This has proven to be true when the *Star Wars* movies came about right up to today's films. Another top moneymaker was G. I. Joe, making over $19 million in spite of sales lost due to production shortage. G. I. Joe was the first action figure to be tagged "action figure for boys," with the success of blockbuster films, creative the spin-off license. By 1989, children now had an interactive role in the market playground, such as Ontario Place and Canada's Wonderland; they would do as well as their American cousins. By the 1980s, the computer hit the home market. As computers became smaller and faster and became more accessible, the image of childhood became a blur in the world itself. In my life, in the early years, what was free for viewing, now we must pay big bucks to see special channels, these same shows. Also, it can be purchased in DVD and Blu-ray box sets. Good, you may say, but if you knew the market strategy, your view may change that you had to have it. I don't think they had that in mind. They were just struggling filmmakers and actors trying to make a living. At the time you came about, all was part of the landscape; you thought it was always like that and never ever questioned anything and got everything you wanted.

And by gum, your papa just bought you a new pair of shoes and Bobby, his first wristwatch. Today, you each get your own smartphone.

It started with the baby boom:

> Baby—You can have it now!
> Boom—Times, they are a changing—turn, turn, turn.
> Boom—Generation X and Y and beyond, no sense to what you
> wanted, just we wanted more.

Today, the economic meltdown, BP oil spills, local power outages, and earthquakes.

As this comes to press, this is old news and bigger disasters are to follow.

All is not over yet; there is hope, and the one who can save us is . . . yelps, you! Find out how; the answer is in the final chapter.

Of course, you will have to buy this book for the whole story.

CHAPTER 1

The 1950s

First Girlfriend

My parents and   Me and my mother
my cousins

My cousin, my   Larry, Gram,
aunts, and Gram   and me

Me—Studio shot

It began for me one stormy night when I was born, June 18, 1946, on a Wednesday; they say a Wednesday child is full of woe. I was also part of baby boom generation; we were to be the largest demographic in history, different for the following reasons: Our parents were survivors of the Great Depression and World War II. They were determined that their children would be better and never be without. "After the war, we would be living in a time of affluence. We would be more educated, healthier, more influence, and sophisticated." I remember so well many of the events growing up in the 1950s. My first fight with my first best friend comes to mind. I knocked him flying down a hill in a fight. Years later, I learned his older sister was, in fact, his mother. He lived with his parents and his older sister. His parents turned out to be his grandparents, and his older sister was, indeed, his mother. This was very normal in the 1950s with unwed mothers. And last I heard, my friend became a Royal Canadian Mounted Police (Mountie).

The neighborhood I lived in was very unique. The street where I lived was twice the width than any other streets. We had the milkman making deliveries by horse and wagon with a feed bag. There must be a backstory why the streets were so wide. One of the hills I used to climb was called Nanny Goat Hill. I used to get burrs stuck to my pants as I climbed. In the past, goats used to climb those very hills. When I got my first bike, because my legs were so short, the only way to stop my bicycle was to crash into parked cars. I still have trouble with bikes that are too big for me. And yes, I do crash when the bike is too big for me. The start of my street is now closed off by a big plant. They remain a mystery to me. I must research and find out the story why the street was closed off like that. I lived in a big old house; we listen to radio shows like *The Lone Ranger*, *The Jack Benny Program*, and *Boston Blackie*. Now everyone on the block had a television. We had only two stations, in French and English. This was broadcasted through the CBC (Canadian Broadcasting Corporation). I can even remember the jingle that advertised my black-and-white TV, advertised on the radio, "Better buy a *Crosby*." My whole life then on was focused on TV; it was now my world, and I'm sure it was the same with many.

"Families were now preoccupied with possession. Television became the way of anticipatory socialization. Little did we know it but, this was how we would learn social skills, preparing us to live in this new mobile society." As they said, we now were expected to keep up with the Joneses as our role model would be TV's own programs like *I Love Lucy*, *The Honeymooners*, and *Leave It to Beaver*. This would become the archetype of family programming that would follow, all heavily sponsored and making sure we kids ate the right cereal and our parents drank the right coffee and drove a new Chevrolet. We had our own culture in television's golden age of children's programming. With the CBC, shows like *Howdy Dowdy*, *Mr. Dressup*, and *The Friendly Giant* began in the 1950s, continued in popularity through many decades, and still can be seen in repeats. Greater than them all was a mouse named Mickey. The man running the show was Walt Disney with his market savvy for shows like *The Mickey Mouse Clubhouse* show, Disneyland, and movies like *Old Yeller*, *20,000 Leagues Under the Sea*, his nature films, and my favorite TV show, *Zorro*. All would make us spellbound of the endless possibility of imagination. He would have such an overwhelming influence over our parents decision over buying with the Disney name. Mr. Disney would be the first to pioneer the television market with Davy Crockett's coonskin cap and would be the first to focus on the children's consumer products, further exploring the marvelous, wonderful world of Disney. This would not be the only influence in our lives. What was most important were cowboys like Roy Rogers, king of the cowboys, and Gene Autry. The one that started the consumer craze was *Hopalong Cassidy* (William Boyd). Who would be first of many to purchase the rights just before it appeared on TV and product placement? Before long, there was heavy merchandising of entire outfits, dressing youngsters head to toe as their favorite cowboy or cowgirl star. I can well remember me and one of my cousins having the complete set of Gene Autry double guns with armbands and spurs. Just to show you I was into cowboys, I used to grease my holster. I was sure to be the quickest gun on the block. Next came in school yards, yo-yos, and cards of which I finally won the complete set and then lost all in one play. I was the youngest in the Boy Cubs. I remember my first night exercising; I peed in my pants and was sent home in a taxi. Going to camp was great. When it was time for parents to visit their boys, my friend cried, "I want to go home." This was a terrible place to eat burnt toast and drink Jungle Juice. I screamed, "I want to go home too!" My friend went home with a new baseball. Our parents were angry because they had to spend all this money on our holiday.

I went to camp every summer from ages nine to fourteen; I learned skills such as swimming, canoeing, and row boating—all would last me a lifetime. All these great memories I can easily remember because of tunes like "Hello Muddah, Hello Fadduh," sung by Bobby Sherman. That was a big hit in the 1960s. It was such fun going to the movies. The British films were the best, like *X: The Unknown* and anything with Christopher

Lee and Peter Cushing, along with all the great B movies, Westerns, *The Three Stooges*, and *The Bowery Boys*. All these movies later would be carried over from the 1930s and '40s from our parents' youth. The events in the 1950s, the bigotry, political happenings caused many changes in all our lives. Music now played a big part in what was happening in my life. By 1955, there were two kinds of music playing on the radio, Negro rhythm and blues and white romantic crooning. Most R & B was banned from most radio stations, saying it was far too sexual and aggressive. They would only promote big-name performers like Doris Day, Perry Como, and Frankie Laine. We had no idea all this was happening in the background. With the economic changes, so too would be a shift in the atmosphere, changes not only in America and Britain, but Canada as well. At first, teenagers had nothing that they could call their own—no music, no clothes, nothing that they could identify with; they became angry because of all this. They had money to spend; teens began to riot. With such films as *The Wild One*, starring Marlon Brando (1954) and *Rebel Without a Cause* (1955) starring James Dean, even Michael Landon, from the television show *Bonanza*, got into the act with a movie called *I Was a Teenage Werewolf* (1957). Now businessmen began to see teenagers as a growing new market, and like the children's market, they very quickly relied on it. They had money to spend and had separate needs. Teens now could buy anything that was put in front of them with such gems as motorcycles, jeans, burgers, milkshakes, and most of all—the biggest market—music.

Two names of when you think of the 1950s are Elvis Presley and Marilyn Monroe; despite their iconic fame, both would have the same fate at the end from drug overdose. Elvis would become the King of Rock and Roll; Marilyn would be become the supreme symbol of Hollywood. Both would be the biggest pop icons of all time. In life and death, both would be marketed for their music and movies, for their names and likeness and image. Sales from the children's market climbed even higher as fortunes would be made from such products as Magic Markers, Silly Putty, and Monopoly. By 1959, another product came out to become what would change the lives of little girls everywhere; the name was Barbie. She became the biggest seller of all time. Marketeers were quick to note, as Stephen Kline in his book *Out of the Garden: Toys and Children's Culture in the Age of TV Marketing*, "The campaign revealed that toy makers could borrow heroes from established media and redesign them for their own purpose, retaining control over the identity profile and position." This proves to be true to all decades that followed and beyond. As the 1960s approached, we had no idea what was going to happen next; all we wanted was more toys. This was when the term *generation gap* would pop up in conversation between teens and parents. Teenagers were now becoming individuals.

As to the News Event of the 1950s

The Soviet Union began putting nuclear missiles on submarines. U.S. Senator Joseph McCarthy told President Truman that the State Department is inflicted with Communist sympathizers. This brought about a hunt and back list. The postwar baby boom dramatically increased the birthrate in North America, Europe, Australia, and Asia. There are over 1.5 million television sets. In 1950, the CBS broadcasted the first TV program in color. We had our own form of broadcast in color in Canada, kind of (what I saw for myself). They had four colored stripes (plastic sheet) and placed it over your TV screen. There you have it, folks, colored television! The average North American living wage had skyrocketed, and the labor market had tightened. It all made it possible for us or our parents to buy a house or a car. Canadians bought. It was the age of the cold war, bomb shelters, and Bomarc missiles. Most were felt in the United States than in Canada. It was also the decade of Sputnik (the race for space had begun), Khruschev, and Castro. In the 1950s, the fear of nuclear war was around us. I knew nothing of this, being I was just a kid. This fear was to be shown in such film as Stanley Kubrick's film *Dr. Strangelove or: How I Learned to Stop Worrying and Loved the Bomb* (1964). In the 1950s, it was said we were coasting along while in the '60s, bigger changes to come would change us all socially forever.

CHAPTER 2

The 1960s

Choir Boys, what I looked like in those days.

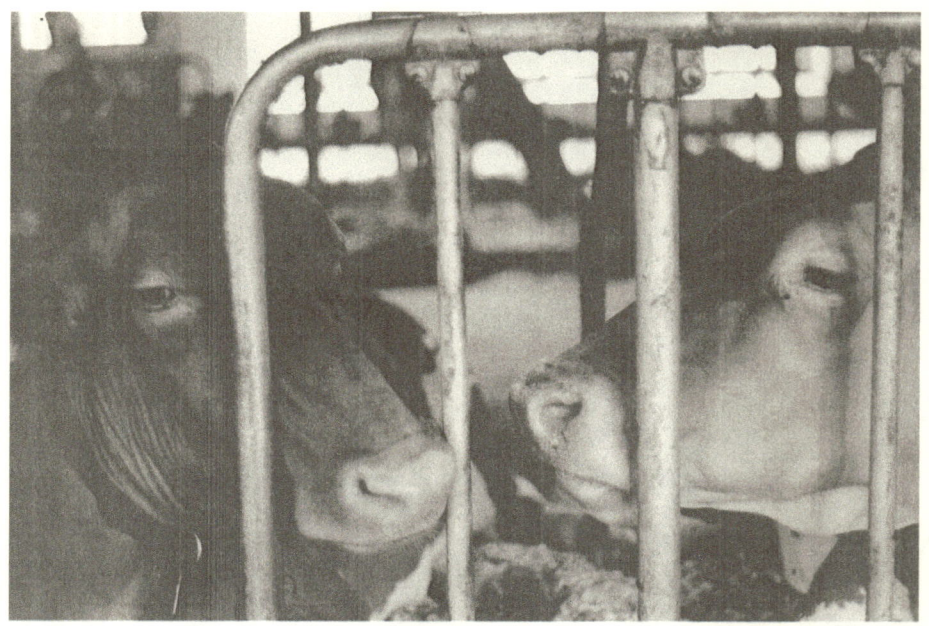

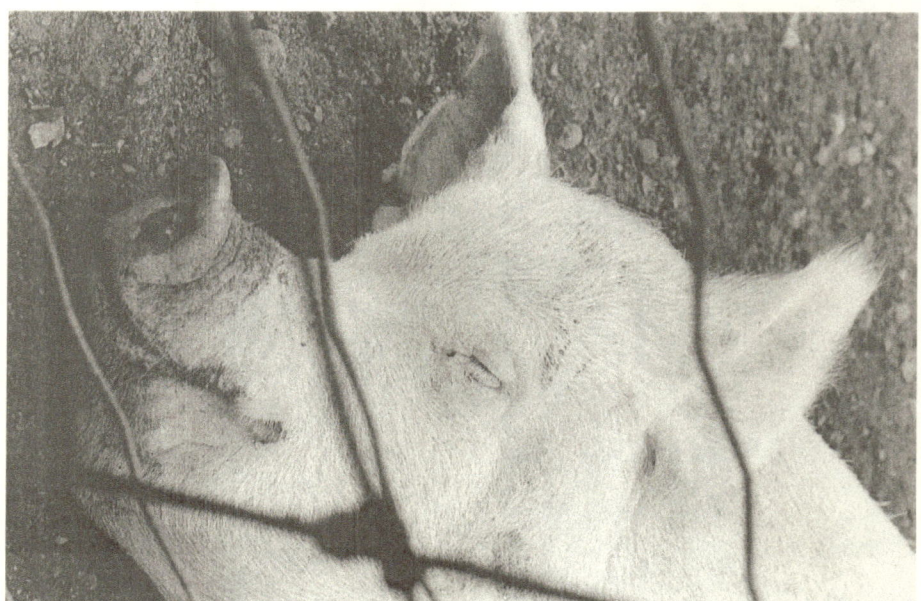

Photography—Farm animals

It was said that the 1960s had challenged the nation's social and political idealism. The biggest change happened when U.S. president Kennedy was assassinated in Dallas, Texas, and the world had lost its incense. Three months later, my dear grandmother died. I can remember trips by bus to the United States. I once got locked in the washroom. I screamed; they had to stop the bus. Or the time we were in New York City, on the fourteenth floor and me in total pitch-black darkness trying to find my way to the washroom. My father told everyone how I almost fell out the window (maybe so). I'm just no good in total darkness! I had many experiences waking up in a different place, and it was total darkness; I (I don`t know where I was) would go around like a blind man, trying to find my way around. Even this year, I can be in a movie theater and one part is in total darkness, and once again, I am feeling lost. I don't think I am no different from anyone else.

The biggest change in the times to us all is with the true joy of music, dance craze, TV, movies, and all the wonderful new products it would bring. This was such a cure to all our fears. Like in the 1950s, toy companies were quick to release toys and games of the latest hit TV show; this was the beginning of a multimillion-dollar ad campaign to promote their products. We were primed and ready. By the 1960s, the target was set for the youth, set forth by the TV image. "So began the phenomenon of TV licensing. With cases full of TV tie-in products." Suddenly kids were going into dime stores and asking for products by name and company. Come on, we all heard of Mattel; you all know the cry, "You can tell it's Mattel, it's swell!" And "It's a wonderful toy—it's Ideal." Other companies were quick to join in the advertising craze—big names such as Milton Bradley, Parker Brothers, Topps, Aladdin, MPC, Transogram, Revell, GAF, Colour Forms, and many other companies. Cartoons were not just for Saturday mornings, but for when you got home from school, with the crazy antics of Yogi Bear, *The Rocky and Bullwinkle Show*, and *Snagglepuss*. Now in cereal boxes, offering prizes, puzzles, masks, and records. Come to think of it, was this not the same promo that our mom got in her box of laundry detergent, finding a full towel inside? Each show that fell under TV entertainment would now be selling coloring books, comics, toys, puzzles, lunch boxes, dolls, and view masters with hit shows like *The Addams Family*, *The Munsters*, *The Monkees*, *Lost in Space*, *The Outer Limits*, *Batman*, and *Star Trek*. All, years later, would become collectables and limited editions. That is another chapter I will be getting into. Years later, many of these classic television shows would become movies that would start a new craze to a whole new generation.

The worse, as I see it, was when you went to places like Disney World, located in Florida. Parents (us baby boomers) now got our kids and the next kids onward to love the Disney characters and worship them and proudly display the Disney logo and wear Mickey Mouse ears. "Wait a minute," you say, "now you're talking about my family." It's just a point of view; this is just the way I see it. You may have thought that yourself. And this was going on years before companies got people to buy their logo on T-shirts, which they proudly displayed logos that gave these companies free advertising. This would all make a lot of people rich; but this, my friend, was where the plot thickens to where we spend our money and where we were more than willing to accept and not question, and the coming generation of kids want and demand these products. And you ask yourself, "How the heck did us consumers fell into this never-ending spending trap?" We just say, "We fell into it with open arms and a bigger shopping bag."

Then there was music. It started first with the great music of the 1950s, with country music, doo-wop, and the outstanding hit makers—Chuck Berry, Ray Charles, Elvis Presley, and Buddy Holly. In the 1960s, it started with what they called bubblegum music, along with the Motown empire, all the wonderful girl groups, and novelty records like The Chipmunks, "Purple People Eater," and "They're Coming to Take Me Away, Ha-Haaa." All the one-hit wonders—the English invasion with the Beatles along with the top bands leading the way, such as The Beach Boys, The Birds, Monkees, Sam Cooke, The Rolling Stones (which the English called the Rolling Uglys), and James Brown. Years later, this was to be known as the golden oldies; to marketers, it would be a never-ending pot of gold, a cash cow.

Not all the star makers made fortunes. Mostly, the record companies made the most money. It would take many years before these groups made their money and became *icons*. In all, we kids, and now teens, were buying the records, dancing with the entire dance craze with "The Twist" and mashed potato. I went to the school dance, dancing up a storm to the "Monster Mash." All this great music would come to haunt me in exercise class. And now we pay top dollar to companies in late-night infomercials that have all been remastered, all ready to relive those glory days of music. I have many of these records, but there is nothing like hearing a remastered version of these songs on a good sound system, with technology that reinvents itself, going into different formats—all costing more and more money to be spent. "All is good," you say; yes, but kids are getting deaf sooner.

Every weekend, I danced to local bands that were so good. When I danced, I always put on a show. With the sound of The Rolling Stones and The Yardbirds, I had the greatest fun. My cousins were real hell-raisers; oh, the trouble they caused. My fun with them began when we were kids. Every weekend, they would come down to my place. They were Larry, Gary, and Ken—the three stooges. On Friday nights, we would watch horror movies on TV, Shock Theatre, with a headless Dave Patrick announcing the next movie, such films from the past like *Island of Lost Souls*. Whenever they would say something crazy, we would repeat the same line: "Are we not men? We beast." Gary would say, "Me not animal, me beast!" We would all say, "Me beast!" The next morning, we made boiled bologna sandwiches and made experiments with balloons. For the trouble they caused, they would leave the bus and throw firecrackers in the driver's window—*bang, bang, be-bang*—and run home. Then the police would come knocking on the door; I would be hiding in the washroom. They used to drive their next-door neighbor crazy. Gary would set a plastic model car on fire. Poor Mrs. Bunchier would scream. Gary would call out, "Go ahead, call the police, and tell them we set a car on fire!" Gary would also wash his jeans with bleach, and they would come out with patches of white, looking like cowhide. Crazy bastard. My cousins were crazy about chocolate milk; they used to collect bread wrappers to get prizes.

They went on to form their own musical group; I was their equipment manager, and I also got them gigs—that is another story. Oh, the trouble they caused, much of which I better not talk about as it would get us all in shit. It was a great time I had with them, all of which we all can recall the events with great affection of the times. It was the greatest of times; it was the worst of times. By 1967, it was called the Summer of Love. It was also one of discontent and rebellion. It was a time of people living in communes and becoming hippies and growing long hair. The youth would march in the street to protest the war and a call for civil rights. It was also the time people experimented with LSD; the Beatles used it, making their music even more inventive. I never took drugs; I just knew enough to know that this had nothing to do with what I wanted in my life. The time they were a changing, at one point, I remember seeing the national news; the newscaster said, "If you use drugs, this is very bad. But if you do drugs and needles, this is the proper way to do it!"

I loved the music of the times, not what was going on.

Film. The highest grossing film of the twentieth century was *The Sound of Music*; other blockbuster films were *Psycho* (the shower scene always made my blood run cold), *Breakfast at Tiffany's*, *Hard Day's Night*, and so many more Oscar-winning movies The longest-running film series that made the largest amount of money and made the biggest impression was a gentleman spy called James Bond. The beginning would always be the same: The screen would go black; a pulsing staccato beat would fill the theater. A series of white dots would march across the screen in rhythm to the music. One would grow in size, and we would find ourselves suddenly looking down a telescopic sight. A man drops to one knee and fires directly at us. A red veil would slowly descend over the screen, and the telescope sight would begin to waver, then sag downward, shrink, and it would once again be a white dot. The film audience all over the world would expect to see a bigger-than-life adventure, gadgets, beautiful women, an evil villain out to take over the world, and a superspy who everyone wishes they could be.

Fashion. The Beatles had the biggest influence on young men's fashion and hairstyle, noted for their mop-top haircuts and Nehru jackets. The bikini came into fashion in 1963 after being feature in the movie *Beach Party*. The miniskirt became the rage in the late 1960s. Women's hairstyles ranged from beehive hairdos and, as the decade ended, by shorter style of Twiggy.

Happenings in the News

1960

The first debate for a presidential election was televised. It was between Senator John F. Kennedy and Richard M. Nixon. Nixon seemed nervous, but Kennedy stood tall. The debate on TV changed many people's minds about Kennedy.

This year, NASA sent up Echo, the first communications satellite to be seen with the naked eye.

American U2 spy plane was shot down over the USSR.

The Olympic Games were held in Rome, and Wilma Rudolf won three gold medals.

1961

John F. Kennedy moved into the White House. He gave his famous speech, "Ask not what your country can do for you, but what you can do for your country."

The Soviets sent the first man into space, and the Americans needed a man in space too. The event came on May 5, 1961. Alan Shepard was sent to space in the *Freedom 7*. On May 25, Kennedy wanted to have a man on the moon and back before the decade was over.

1962

John Glenn became the first man to orbit the earth three times. It was a five-hour flight.

Rachel Carson, a scientist and writer, warned that our earth would die of pollution and chemicals, especially chemicals that were developed to kill bad insects. DDT was a really bad chemical. It killed bad insects along with good insects, plants, and animals. She wrote the book *Silent Spring* with a warning. At least five states banned DDT.

1963

Martin Luther King Jr. made the speech, "I have a dream," on August 28, 1963. More than two hundred thousand peaceful demonstrators came to Washington DC to demand equal rights for blacks and whites. Part of the speech was "I have a dream that my four little children will one day live in a nation where they will not be judged by the color of their skin but by the content of their character."

President Kennedy was assassinated in Dallas, Texas, on November 22. Kennedy's assassin, Lee Harvey Oswald, was never sent to trial. While being moved by police to a different jail, a man named Jack Ruby shot Oswald. Who killed President Kennedy? Nobody knows for sure.

1964

The Beatles, a British rock and roll band, became *very* popular. The Fab Four—John, Paul, George, and Ringo—were played on radio stations all over the world. They were seen on the *Ed Sullivan Show*. They performed concerts that were quickly sold out. All the frenzy over the group became known as Beatlemania, which was only the beginning.

This was the first year the cigarette boxes had a warning printed on it: "Smoking can be hazardous to your health." It had not occurred to the U.S. government to give the warning that smoking led to cancer and lung problems.

The first civil rights bill was passed to stop racial discrimination.

1965

President Johnson ordered bombing raids on North Vietnam, and Americans began protesting the war.

The world's first roofed stadium was built—the Houston Astrodome.

1966

Walt Disney, the creator of Mickey Mouse and a pioneer of animated films, died of cancer on December 15, 1966, but his legend lives on.

1967

The first heart transplant was performed by Dr. Christiaan Barnard in Cape Town, South Africa.

1968

Civil rights leader Martin Luther King was assassinated in Memphis, Tennessee. Two months later, Robert Kennedy, John F. Kennedy's brother, was assassinated too. Both were civil rights leaders.

On November 5, 1968, Shirley Chisholm was elected America's first black woman to Congress.

1969

Nearly half a million people headed over to a six-hundred-acre farm in New York for the Woodstock Festival. Many top rock musicians were there. It lasted three days, a weekend of music, love, and peace.

July 20, 1969, 4:18 p.m., one of the biggest events of history happened. *Apollo 11* landed on the moon, astronauts aboard. Neil Armstrong's famous speech for the historical steps, "That's one small step for man, one giant leap for mankind."

As the decade came to a close, everything had to reinvent itself; man had gone to the moon, and after a while, it was sad, no big deal. The 1970s would bring about even more change; for me, it was the best decade ever as one of great discovery and action.

CHAPTER 3

The 1970s

Danger Film Location

My best friend and his cousins

One of my tease girl friends

I was a film extra in this movie

Photography—Horse in field

Canada day amazement

Terry, the happiest guy in the World, my friend said

My friend, as James Bond, bond poster shots

Terry on frozen lake

Me, filming in action

Me, in action pose

In air field, as it happened

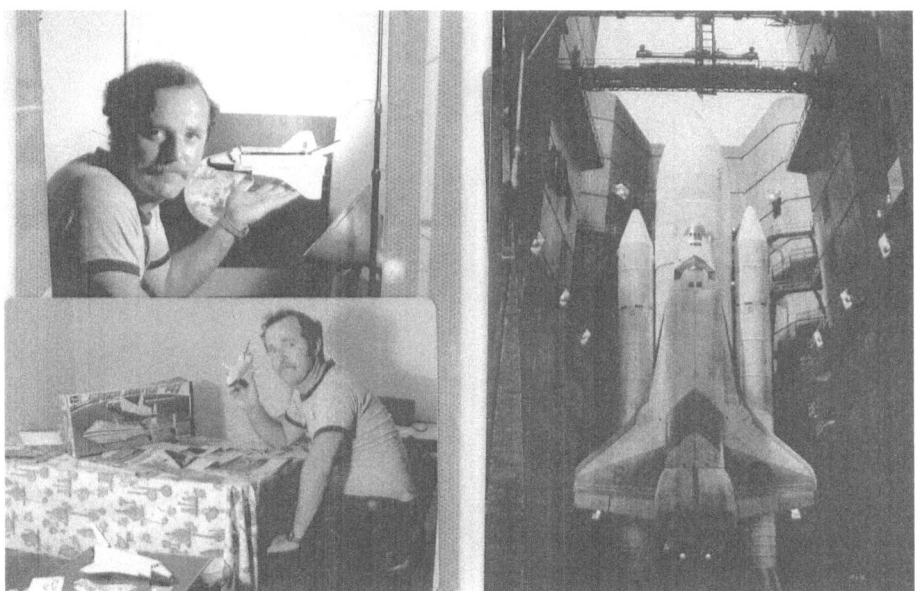

Filming behind the scenes

Terry Bond enters the space race

Angle shot of real Rocket,
location Science Museum—Ottawa

Me, Self Portrait

There were new changes in technology, fashion, movies, and music. The Beatles just broke up and formed their own musical groups; my cousins all got married, and the world opened up for me. This was where I became the person I am today. I got into photography and filmmaking and started collecting, first with James Bond stuff. The changes started with getting a new job, meeting new people, getting involved, and lots of self-discovery. Of all the decades, this was my favorite. One in which I made many lifelong friendships. Music played a big part in all this. This was the sound track as you drove your car. I got a used Datsun and drove it for three years. I only paid $1,400. I also got a super 8mm camera, a moviemaking kit, and a movie projector. All of which I got on a bank loan. So the money cycle began. You got to spend money if you want to get exactly what you want. The movies in the 1970s were the best ever. All kept you on the edge of your seat—films like *Jaws, The Exorcist, E. T., Star Wars*, and a new James Bond, Roger Moore. We were all working and spending money, having the time of our lives. You boomers, did you have a similar experience? Or did you jump and get married and start a new family? Music now, in the 1970s, was just what you listened and danced to. You went to concerts. It was an event; it was a happening.

The performers and groups, such as Alice Cooper and The Who, put on high-tech shows with lasers and theater productions—a good time for my friends who smoked up grass, or weed. I still do not do it, and I saw all the craziness the people did and the effect years later (I was just laughing so hard). Sometime thirty years later, I will not be here in this life to judge, but it all was a lot of fun. I did drink with my buddies and many things I do not regret. I did it from when I was eighteen years old till my thirties. And this, I would say, goes on at any decade that you grow up in; it's all fun and oh so experience you lives it all. My new friends I met through work, I hung out with, and their parents had a cottage. I lived with them. Their friend was their cousin just like I had as a kid and in my teens. These guys were all were very smart university students, all very insane dudes. For two years, we went to pubs, drank till three o'clock in the morning, played cards, got drunk, scuba dived, and went back to work, sometimes throwing up at the side of the road. I did that for two years straight and had the time of my life.

Again, I say, it is so important you do all this. They got me waterskiing (got this on super 8mm film), driving a car on a frozen lake, making the waterskiing jump, and skiing just for the summer (again, I got photos of all this craziness). At one time, I got a call at 3:00 a.m. to come and save them. "One guy went over a bridge with his car, can you help me?" I am not the smartest guy in the world, but I don't do any crazy ass stuff like that. Or (the same) drunken friend, swimming across the lake. I loved them all (having done that kind of opens up your life to all kinds of possibilities even if you don't realize it till thirty years later). I did many things on my own, got into filmmaking, acting, and starring in other people's movies. It was such a time for one's own self-discovery. Some people I met up with went on to chase their dreams; I was just very happy to be part of the process. What did I want for me? I did not know. It would take me many years to find out; all I have done was, in fact, to be everything I can be. That's okay; I was very smart that I had documented most of what I did and am very proud of all that I was involved in. I just figured I had so many fears, and many people in my family kept me at bay. Lucky for me, I kept all my films no matter what everyone thought. We all spent all kinds of money through the years, but you many so little you not dare step out of the cycle. But these days, one can get in debt faster, and society expects and demands you to do so. That's okay; you always move on, live through a whole new time period. No matter what I (you) did and experienced, it would always be with me (you). And that follows with some fear and regret, and sometimes, it will catch up with you. Me, I was always looking for my own answers, read and experience, and finding my own set of truth. But always, I still went out and did exactly what I set out to do. Silly me, such a silly guy.

The big events of the seventies, in the news, were the association with Vietnam and Watergate. By April 1970, President Nixon ordered U.S. forces into North Vietnam to destroy the supply center; this made riots with every college campus was the most distraction. America celebrated Earth Day for the first time and still continues today. President Nixon was impeached in 1974 due to the lies and abstraction in present. This was known as the Watergate scandal. In 1977, Jimmy Carter was elected as the president of the United States.

In entertainment, popular movies of the decade were the following:

Jaws, with three sequels, and *Star Wars*, with two out-of-the-world sequels, more following ten years later with spin-off movies and a TV series. Alfred Hitchcock's *Psycho* was made after *North By Northwest*, a low-budget horror movie to end all horror movies. *Back to the Future*, which made Michael J. Fox go from a TV star to a movie star. A film ahead of its time, *A*

Clockwork Orange. There were also many great horror movies and teenage films that set the standard for decades to come.

It was these movies that inspired me into making my own movies and opened up the mind of many moviegoers where the movies could bring them. As the technology changed and grew, we all got these moves in Beta, VHS, laser disk, DVD, Blu-ray. And soon, the *Star Wars* saga to be brought out in 3-D.

Top Grossing Movies of the 1970s
Star Wars, 1977; *Jaws*, 1975; *Superman*, 1978; *The Godfather: Part II*, 1974; *One Flew Over the Cuckoo's Nest*, 1975; *Taxi Driver*, 1976; and *French Connection*, 1971.

Popular TV Shows
All in the Family, *M*A*S*H*, *Happy Days*, *Mork & Mindy*, *Six Million Dollar Man*, *The Brady Bunch*, and *Wonder Woman*.

Popular Toys Played With
Slinky, Nerf balls, and Lego.

Popular Music
Fleetwood Mac, ABBA, ELO (Electric Light Orchestra), Deep Purple, Yes, Santana, Supertramp, Kiss, The Moody Blues, Grand Funk Railroad, Alice Copper, Jethro Tull, plus many more that would set the tone and excitement for this decade. All these music excited me into doing all the things I like, and in fact, it's what kind of drives my passion in what really excites me. Let us not forget the wonderful sound track of all our favorite movies. We all had to have that. And for sure, we all started to go to the concerts. Music was much more than you just listened to.

Fads and Fashion
Tie-dye T-shirts, bell-bottoms, disco suits with gold chain—all the usual that were always worn while going to the club. I went there once. (Been there, done that.) lava lamps, shag rugs, Pet Rock. On Earth Day, people always planted a tree.

Muscle Cars
Ford Mustang, Dodge Charger, Cadillac, Eldorado convertible, Buick Century Turbo Coupe, and the Volkswagen.

1970 Big Inventions

In 1971, the data matrix was invented; the food processor and liquid crystal display was made, and the VCR (video cassette recorder).

By 1972, the word processor was invented. In 1975, the laser disk came out. By 1976, the first ink-jet printer was invented. In 1979, cell phones came out—do you remember how big it was?

CHAPTER 4

The 1980s

Me, Bean Bond

Best Dogs of My Life

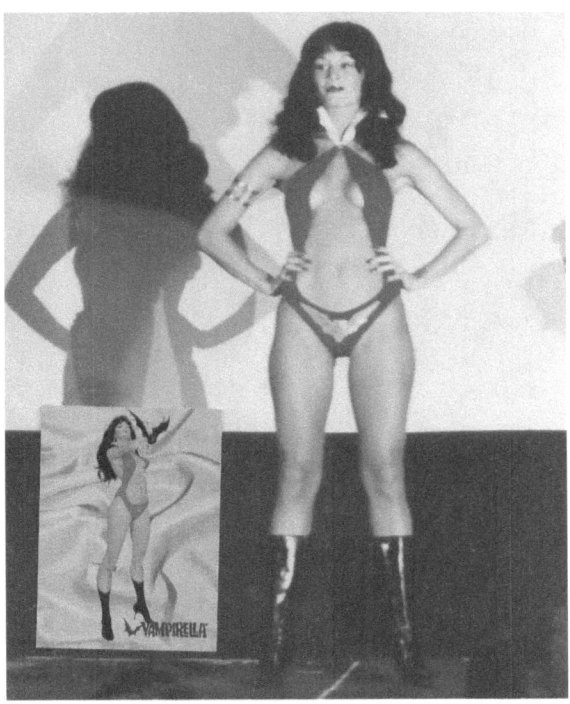

Photography—Vampirella N.Y.

Filming on location

Self portrait of me, as Bond, photo made with Photoshop

By 1980, two of my very good friends that opened the world to me had moved to Toronto. They said, "You should move down here because everything you love so much is here, come live with us." I had been to Toronto before in past visits. I had gone down for a Super 8mm Film Festival, so I had ideas what the place was like. I agreed, packed my bags, and quit my job. I did not have a job waiting for me. Somehow, I got a job at a university, in a kitchen. I got another job offer two weeks later; it was at a film reproduction lab as a shipper receiver. My friend, who I starred in his movies, moved down to Hollywood to chase his dream! I remember so well; he said to himself that he had no choice. I had to do it! I don't think I told you, I have a lifelong speech problem. I never let anything stop me live my life; some days were just harder than others. At the interview, the person interviewing me would tell you, "He opened his mouth and nothing came out."

I remember everything so well. I guess he liked my eagerness and hired me. I got back to the other job, made up a story, and told them. It was 100 percent BS, and they said, "Okay," and "You better be on your way." I stepped into my new job; this was in September 1980. I started to take some courses at George Brown College in 16mm basic filmmaking and audio production. I had a great time and had lots of fun; everyone loved me so much, and I fit in. I worked hard at work, had lots of fun. Of course, I had many troubles on the phone calling the curriers, but I know enough that I had to do it. Then two years later, my friends went on a bicycle trip to Europe, and I kept myself busy at work and took the advance course in 16mm filmmaking. It was fun, and I filmed many gems, but I did not really want to be a filmmaker—or so I thought. I just figured I had so many fears; it would stop me. I also took four cooking courses—basic and advance, bread making, and Chinese cooking. I picked up many new skills. Again, I did not really want to work in a kitchen, having had some real-world experience. I still made film on my own with a new friend; it was another James Bond film. This time I would play 007. The action was at the Scarborough Bluffs. A great location with cliffs around and the top of the hill drops off. The shore was down below. I made up a story where this guy thought he was James Bond. There was someone out to get him. He was having a fight on the cliffs; meanwhile, there was a jet flying overhead. A rope dropped down, and he grabbed it. The bad guy tried to grab him but fell to his death and landed on the seashore. That was a managed production but had its faults. I was we pretty exciting I even tried to do. I ended up with four versions of the movie. I entered it into a film contest but did not win.

The problem with my films was it had too much copyright music. I used all Bond music, and it was very exciting. But as always, it all gets pushed under the rug; but I was smart enough to know what I liked and saved everything. For many years, I took a backseat. I always believed in myself no matter what anyone had to say. I got asked by a film teacher to come back into the film course; my film feature knew how much fun I was having, and I did not have to pay for it. My teacher gave me his 16mm camera and told me to do some film on my own. I just got connected with some friends and got those excited to write and film, and we would get the class involved. We did it for a bit, but I dropped out; my friend was out of control and knew enough to get out. As the decade ended, I took an advance course in scuba diving at a night school where we did ice diving, then went to a frozen lake and practiced everything we learned. I filmed the whole thing on video as always to document all I do. Later that summer, I got another part-time job and worked another thirty hours. By the end of the fall, I had a heart attack. That is another story, another book to write. What saved me in all this were some of the valuable lessons I learned in night school, something that was on one of my final questions. "What would you. Answer too (something like that)." The correct answer was, you answer was you answer was, you answer to yourself. So when I had trouble, I go to the people; that's where, that is the job to help you. And it worked for me every time I applied that knowledge, "fur through, I got the help fast, in every situation. By December, I was in the hospital for thirteen days. I was in Intensive Care for one week; I did see the bright light. I did not die; I just did exactly what the doctors told me, 100 percent to the letter. At the end of the decade, going into the next, as always, not missing a beat!

"Wait a minute," you say, "wasn't the book about consumer spending?" Yes, it is, but it is my story of what was happening, and as you soon learned at each chapter end, all the new things that came about throughout technology, music, movies, and fashion trends. I would because I was always making very little; I had to be very resourceful, which I still am. Stick with me, and you will learn a lot and have fun in the process.

History

The decade started off with a bang in the form of both natural and man-made disasters, including the eruption of Mount St. Helens and the assassination of John Lennon; Ronald Reagan was elected toward the end of the year, the beginning of his almost decade-long reign as the leader of the free world. Music got a shakeup as well with a move away from disco and song singer of the 1970s. New sounds hit the airwaves in the form of Blondie, Devo, and The Sugarhill Gang with something new—rap. Millions of TV viewers wanted the answers to one question: who shot J. R.?

This was the beginning of the era, the '80s. I can remember when rap hit the airwaves through the media; the public quickly gaped it out, and new super rap stars came out and are still with us. Fortune was made and is still being made. People forgot its roots started back in the 1980s. For sure, there was a story there and how the record companies made their money. For me, the memories of the 1980s are very vivid—the sound of the music, the fashion. Everyone had big hair, usually the band, and the music was very loud and heavy. It was the time rock video started, as well as TV stations such as Citytv and MuchMusic. And new TV specialty networks sprung up—such as MTV, CNN, the Family Channel, and the Disney Channel. Soon to follow were Bravo, HGTV, CBC News, CTV News, TSC, Canada's own YTV, and all kinds of movie networks. Now everyone got cable and satellite dishes. Quickly everyone got a video player/recorder, coming in Beta, VHS. There was a format war, which would be the standard, and VHS won. The video player came, soon followed by the video camera recorder. It was big and very chunky. You had to have a car to transport the recorder. Movies, for the first time, came out for sale and rent. I remember, for rental, you had to put down $100 as deposit for each video. I had saved a few magazine shows on all that was available. It was all very costly, but we all had to have it in our home. New electronic stores came up; as the technology grew, so too did the store. I was one of the first to rent a video machine. Usually, if you got the first model out, it cost $1,399. Never mind the cost; we all bought it. Spend, spend, baby. Then there were video games with Pac-Man and Donkey Kong, Nintendo. This began the video game industry. It would make more money than the movie industry and outgrow, in time, prime movies. Then there were the kids; how quickly they became addicted to all this. I'm sure there were plenty of kids that dropped out of school because of this.

But that is cool; it was all good for the economy.

The new *Star Wars* came out—*The Empire Strikes Back*, and *Return of the Jedi*. Pretty soon you got the complete video set of the *Star Wars* saga. Better sound systems came to movie theaters with THX and IMAX. Now moviegoing was an event. You got music to buy, concerts to see. New theme parks came about, which first started with California Disneyland.

In Canada, we got our own version—Canada's Wonderland and Ontario Place. I do not have the date of the start-up, but I'm sure it was around the same time.

The travel industry exploded; many packed their bags and packsacks and explored the world. Coming back, which I'm pretty sure of, were such fads as tattoos and skin sparing. I'm sure there are some to set me straight. I'm very sure this was where this all came about. But its roots go much farther back to the 1940s and '50s, in the war year.

Everyone was sure to remember soldiers coming back with tattoos on their arms. I think it started out with people being drunk and taking dares. It is still very much the fashion, but I wonder to myself, to your people now, where this all came about. New she was an industry to come about, which I got into; that is for collectors with limited editions. Whatever you love, most movies and music, now you can get an action figure. It started first with Barbie and G. I. Joe and *Star Wars* figures and comics. First addition is now with a further. I remember how kids bought comics and action figures as an investment for their retirement fund for their old age. This was another spending madness that began. I got into collecting James Bond items and toys for the 1970s and '80s, going to collector shows. I still have a large collection in large boxes. For many, this was the beginning of huddling, but its roots—why people keep and collect things—go much farther back. Again, more of my money to spend, but it is and was fun. As they say, it's about the "hunt." So too became the roots of making their own magazine called ZINS. Sports got quickly on the bandwagon with WWF wrestling; this too became a megaindustry and still is. New stores changed such as Toys "R" Us, Future Shop, and Best Buy. Again, I do not have the dates when things all came about, but be sure, it was all about the same time.

Note to the reader: I am not an expert; just like you lived all things. I just dared to ask the question, "Hey, what just happened here?" And again, so much happens in the new and with the economy, everything's change. As they say, the more things change, the more it remains the same.

Top Grossing Movies of the '80s

Star Wars: The Empire Strikes Back—1980
The Blues Brothers—1980
Romancing the Stone—1984
Ghost Busters—1984

Beetle Juice—1988
Ferris Bueller's Day Off—1986
Big—1988
The Abyss—1989
Nine to Five—1980
Flashdance—1983
Arthur—1981
The Terminator—1984
Footloose—1984
Cocoon—1985
Raiders of the Lost Ark—1981
All these film I've seen many times and, in later years, got copies in
    VHS and DVD.

Famous People Who Died in the 1980s

Alfred Hitchcock
Peter Sellers
Steve McQueen
John Lennon

CHAPTER 5

1990s

IT'S WAR!—What I saw when I
got home from the hospital

Best Summer of My Life

Film making idea, on the roof

In the country, it was the best of times, and the worst of times

I kind of consider this decade as my lost years, not really as I did quite a bit; I remember I was always working. As I told you, what happened at the end of 1980s, I was in the hospital; I was there for thirteen days. The way I looked at everything may well be different than most, being true to my feelings. As I told people, I had a heart attack; at any point in time, they were shocked. Being as I was there and I lived it, I think it's important to educate people. First off, it happened to me when I was forty-four, and compared to my mother's heart attack when she was in her sixties, it hit her worse. The doctor at the hospital said that there is no such thing as a small heart attack. My feelings were, "Wow, I never felt like this before." The way I handled the situation was good; in most of my night-school courses, I got educated in handling any emergency. The best thing I learned was go to the right people for help because that's their job. When I applied this knowledge, fur flew. The right action was taken as was well taken care of. It was funny; I thought the doctor in charge called my work to tell them I would not be in. He just called my work, did not tell them who he was; he just said, "In behalf of Terry Brownlee, he will not be in!" Wow, so blunt—a man of action.

Anyways, I was so well taken care of in the hospital. It was such an event in my life. Later, when I got home, I recorded the event on video. On the way home, I picked up the newspaper. This was the beginning of a new year, a new decade. The front page read: IT'S WAR! Everything in the world and everyone's life was affected because of this world event. This time it was the Gulf War. I knew nothing of world events, but it sure affected many people. As it was stated in the Internet: "A companion of factors including the mass mobilization of capital markets thought Neoliberalism, the beginning media such as the Internet and the dissolution of the end of the cold war, with the collapse of the Soviet Union." All this and much more would affect the status of the free world. What was on television every night broadcasted live the Gulf War. Too much information. Such a time; people today just want to forget it even happened. For me, I was safe in my apartment. My roommate just moved out. And within a month, I found a new apartment. What I learned of being on my own, I get very smart really fast and always take quick action. I apply this same method in these days. It works!

Crazy Fads

The gamut—from the grunge to those annoying fanny packs and more body piercing. Furbies, Beanie Babies, electronic Giga Pets—wassup, with related links.

BBC Cult Hits

An archived television series featuring video clips and a skewed look at the Wonderbra, trouser madness, Laura Croft (she is still with us, love) and Viara, Beavis and Butt-Head, Teletubbies, and more pop icons of the decade.

History Moment of 1990–2000

Featuring audio clips of the American decade's famous political speeches, news and sport broadcasts, along images of Bill and Monica, Ross Perot and the Y2K paraphernalia.

Y2K in 1999

A neat snapshot of how computer nerds and risk managers faced the threatening new millennium. We got a six-month warning of the worst disaster in history to happen as the clock struck 12:00 a.m. in the year 2000. Because a cliché in the making of computers, it would not recognize the year 2000, causing (they said) all power problems—airplanes would come crashing to the ground, hospitals would stop functioning, and on and on. We were told, by the TV specials, to store food and water, stock up, and put our savings in a safe place. One financial adviser told everyone to sell everything! I fell a lot of bad advice was given.

What happened at the night of January 1 at 12:00 a.m.? I was at a restaurant at a New Year's Eve party; the band was playing, and the clock struck 12:00 a.m. Everyone cheered and kissed and danced; two minutes later, it suddenly went black—aha, uh-oh! What just happened! We were in total darkness. Was it true? Did it really happen? Did the world come to an end as promised? Within ten minutes, the power went on. The restaurant had played a cruel joke on us all. Everyone was so relieved. The good thing about this event, the power in charge of all the services fixed up all the problems that could happen, and the world, once again, was out of danger. A good lesson to be learned anytime is not to take any doom and gloom as to the truth. Just act on what can be done to make things safer in your life, back up your computer, etc.

The 1990s Greatest Hits

1. "Electric Boogie" (a.k.a. "Electric Slide")—Marcia Griffiths
2. "Ice Ice Baby"—Vanilla Ice

3. "U Can't Touch This"—MC Hammer
4. "I Want to Be Rich"—Calloway
5. "Humpty Dance"—Digital Underground
6. "Here and Now"—Luthor Vandross
7. "Vogue"—Madonna
8. "Pump Up the Jam"—Technotronic
9. "Blaze of Glory"—Jon Bon Jovi
10. "Step by Step"—New Kids on the Block
11. "Everybody Everybody"—Black Box
12. "Here We Are"—Gloria Estefan
13. "She Ain't Worth It"—Glenn Medeiros
14. "Groove Is in the Heart"—Deee-Lite
15. "That's What I Like"—Jive Bunny ('50s medley)
16. "Tom's Diner"—Suzanne Vega feat DNA
17. "From a Distance"—Bette Midler
18. "This Old Heart of Mine"—Rod Stewart and Ronald Isley
19. "Just a Friend"—Biz Markie
20. "Cherry Pie"—Warrant
21. "Love Will Lead You Back"—Taylor Dayne
22. "All My Life"—Linda Ronstadt and Aaron Neville
23. "The Way You Do the Things You Do"—Ub40
24. "Black Velvet"—Alannah Myles
25. "Get Up! (Before The Night Is Over)"—Technotronic

My only comment is, yes, the music was great, but it did have the lasting impact of 1950s-1970s.

TV Shows in 1991

Americans Funniest Videos, In Living Color, Magyer, *Murphy Brown, The Simpsons,* and *The Fresh Prince of Bel-Air.*

Year 1998-99: *Melrose Place, The Nanny, 3rd Rock from the Sun, Friends,* and *Fantasy Island*

Fads

Slang—Back-in-the-day expressions, years ago, in my young days.
Bling—wearing nice jewelry.
The boom—par expect, out of control
Bunk—crazy, out of control

As the decade ended, at my job, in the early 1990s, we were hit by a recession. As the government of that day announced "The recession is over," that's when it really kicked in. My hour was cut in half; I had only twenty-two and a half hours. I could not get UIC unemployment because I had too many hours. I got all kinds of bad advice to either fight it or just stick it out. Right or wrong, I stuck with it, still keeping my apartment, putting money away with RSP (savings). Through the years, it was hard, but it made me very resourceful, being able to live on very little. A very important skill for any time you live through.

CHAPTER 6

Decade of 2000

Here is the short list of what happened in the decade:

- 2000—Y2K fear passes; Bush is elected as president through Supreme Court decision.
- 2001—9/11 attacks; the beginning of war on terror.
- 2002—
- 2003—The beginning of war in Iraq.
- 2004—Bush is reelected as president.
- 2005—Hurricane Katrina leaves Louisiana devastated, kills 1,800 people.
- 2006—Space shuttle discovery lifts off at night, first shuttle launch since 2003.
- 2007—Virginia Tech shooting.
- 2008—Election of Barack Obama; the official beginning of recession.
- 2009—Inauguration of Barack Obama.

Ten Top Gadgets of the Decade
1. The iPod: I just picked up the latest iPod Nano; here are its features:
    I just got a new toy, the Apple iPod Nano. I had an MP3 player before and knew what it could do (compress sound and picture). This had more features; it had a camera, video/audio recorder, and FM radio. You can tag a song on radio and get stuff from podcast. There are many colors and sizes and models to choose from.

2. The GPS device: At first, it was for the car; this day, it has so many uses. There is even one for people on bicycles and campers and travelers. A great new toy, but it also has caused a lot of accidents. If used correctly, it can be a real aid. Some features:

3. The BlackBerry: The BlackBerry is a phone, but this device is like having a mobile office. It was introduced in 1991 as a pager, then into the smartphone it is today. Each year, more features are added.

4. Digital camera: By the year 2000, millions of folks got one of these; now everyone has one. When I got mine two years ago, the price was a bit steep; now cameras are lower in cost and has many features.

5. TiVo digital recorder: TiVo pioneered the device in 1997, but it was in 2000 that the ad-skipped deck really took off, sending advertisers and television programmers back to their drawing board. LG now offered a DV integrated, and serous cable providers provided PVR recorders.

6. Wii: When first introduced, Nintento caused the Wii and Wii Sports in 2006. Using a controller, a player can simulate actions and play games such as hockey, golf, bowling, exercise, as well as teach new skills to all ages.

7. The USB flash device: Known by many names, the memory stick serves as much needed storage for mountains of information, music, audio, and graphics on a mini scale.

8. The iPhone: In June 2007, many die-hard fans of Apple grabbed up the first phones, and within seventy-four days, Apple sold over 1 million of its new devices. It is said now the best iPhone and iPod have sold over 40 million. As this book comes to press, the numbers have surpassed that.

9. E-readers: Sony Readers and Amazon Kindle have gained popularity in novels, newspapers, and magazines; research from Forrester said 2009 was a breakout year, with e-readers and e-books having sales of 176 percent of the year.

10. Netbooks: Smaller and cheaper than its cousins, the laptop and desktop, the netbook has emerged as an increasingly popular PC option. The netbooks, or mininotebooks, can't compete with fully functional laptops and desktops when it comes to memory, power, and battery life. But they can be had for below $300, a price closer to that of some smartphones than traditional computers. In addition to the price, their compact size and mobility makes them attractive options for consumers.

Ten Top Movies of the Decade

1. *Lord of the Rings: The Fellowship of the Ring*
2. *Lord of the Rings: The Return of the King*
3. *Up*
4. *United 93*
5. *The Incredibles*
6. *WALL-E*
7. *Crouching Tiger, Hidden Dragon*
8. *The Dark Knight*
9. *Lord of the Rings: The Twin Towers*
10. *The Wrestler*

Ten Top Songs of the Summer of 2001

1. "Hanging by a Moment"—Lifehouse
2. "Let Me Blow Your Mind"—Gwen Stefani
3. "Drops of Jupiter"—Train
4. "Peaches & Cream"—Puff Daddy
5. "Lady Marmalade"—Christina Aguilera
6. "U Remind Me"—Usher
7. "Hit 'Em Up Style (Oops!)"—Blu Cantrell
8. "Ride wit Me"—Nelly
9. "Bootylicious"—Destiny's Child
10. "Get Ur Freak On"—Missy Elliot

Top Invention to Improve Your Life

- Wireless speakers/headphones, Bluetooth
- Virtual keyboard
- Segway Human Transporter
- UTube
- Camera/video cell phone
- Digital satellite radio
- Artificial liver

What a decade it has been so far; we just had the worst financial meltdown in decades, and they say another one is just around the corner. Here is the reason it happened:

Causes of the crash:

- *Corporate corruption.* Many companies fraudulently inflated their profits and used accounting loopholes to hide debt. Corporate officers enjoyed outrageous stock options that diluted company stock.
- *Overvalued stocks.* There were numerous examples of companies making significant operating losses with no hope of turning a profit for years to come, yet sporting a market capitalization of over a billion dollars.
- *Day traders and momentum investors.* The advent of the Internet enabled online trading—new, quick, and inexpensive way to trade the markets. This revolution led to millions of new investors and traders entering the markets with little or no experience.
- *Conflict of interest between research firm analysts and investment bankers.* It was common practice for the research arms of investment banks to issue favorable ratings on stocks for which their client companies sought to raise capital. In some cases, companies received highly favorable ratings, even though they were actually in serious financial trouble.
- At home for all of us, we got very sloppy with our own money matters, making too many purchases beyond our own budget. The year began for me in 2001; the company where I had worked for the past twenty years went out of business. They were bought out by a bigger company. They did not upgrade fast enough to the latest technology. And because this company I worked for was just so small, I did not get a severance pay, just $500 if I stuck it out to the end, which was taxed. Within a month, without work, I got working in a restaurant. It did not work out; I got myself in a program called the Job Finders Club. It was five days a week, one month free course. It was a very intense course; we would get in practice job-finding skills. Somehow, with one of the techniques—networking—I got a job. It was for a private-owned members club. I was just one of fifty people for a two-day origination; I made it and was there for eight full, very hard-working years. That is another story, which could fill another book. So many misadventures, so many years of fun and struggle. I sure was not along; I meet people from many countries. In the year 2007, I joined a community garden—so many happy, fun times, good times to get in touch with oneself and meet

many new people from different cultures. I was there in the very early beginning when we dug the ground, young and old alike. The group that started this was called Greenest City. The organizers were so savvy in getting grants and the proper permission. The people (gardeners) I was with were so smart and eager to make it happen. I was quick enough to film and take lots of photos and document all that happened. For me, it all was the greatest time of discoveries (once again). I got an offer at work to take an early retirement. I was two years short of age at sixty-five. My health was suffering due to all the craziness we all had to endure, and the time for the economy got worse for all. I was lucky with my exposure with the garden of living a much simpler life. I quickly jumped at the opportunity and took the retirement. Since this place I had worked for was a corporation, I got a good send-off. They asked me what kind of present I wanted; I choose a Sony Blu-ray player. I knew the model number and everything and gave them a list of movies I wanted. They told me I was going to get a party; they then asked me what kind of cake I would want: "Black Forest, please." On my last day of work, I came to work in a stretch limo and home in the same grand style. Once again, I documented the event; many grand speeches were given. I knew enough that for most people, when they get at the end of their working life, it usually ended with lot of bitterness and regret. I chose not to take that route. Yes, it may be a bit crazy to quit work so early, and money will sure be tight. But the opportunity, and my health, was all worth it; the possibilities were very exciting. Lucky for me, I try not to let people tell me how bad things are and what I cannot do anymore. Maybe you're right, but you know what? I'm going to do it anyway; better let me have my way. Silly guy, yes, sure, but oh very happy.

CHAPTER 7

Back from the Past, the Future Is Ours!

Here you have it, a glimmer into what one baby boomer lived through—the subject of consumer spending and my story. It began by reading a book *Out of the Garden: Toys and Children's Culture in the Age of TV Marketing* by Stephen Kline. This would show how through children programming, its popular culture, advertisers, marketers, and market strategy got us to buy their products. I knew from the beginning that it would be a hard sell to try and give you a heads-up into how we all are doped, conned, and persuaded into wanting you to know how this happened and played a big part in everyone's life at any given age or generation you were part of. As I put it, "When you were born, your story begins!" We all know what happens—the news event of each decade and the popular movies and music. But did you have any ideas how we all (each decade) unfolded? How our spending habits came to be? What were the influences? What and how you drove your parents crazy into buying what you wanted? And your parents themselves, and the buying public itself, into buying their next purchase.

I hope you can see the pattern as I live my life and, I'm sure, yours. You and I are so different, but I'm sure we're very much the same; we just have our own story to tell. I am not here just to stand out and tell you the entire event of my life, but of the events, inventions, and entertainment that had a big effect in all our lives. As you get older, your story changes through time itself. And in the end, you may (if I've done my job) have your own questions and come out of this maybe entertained, have a better understanding where we all have been and where we are going. I have done some research into what I have to say, but as a true Gemini—with my questioning mind, my many talents, but a master of nothing! The future is yours. For many lives, the answer is not so easy; so many people run through our life, for the better and sometimes the worse, with the people around us. Life has too many chances to make things better. I hope any of my findings of what is to follow in the coming technology, what is going to happen in the next coming years, what we must know and understand. I just want to tell you there are so many miracles in our life, and though even in the hard times, we all learn so much as people. My mission in life (when I was fifteen years old) was to find 100 percent happiness. I do this by making tons of mistakes, making so many self-discoveries, having fun in the moment, touching people's lives, and (through the years) forgiving myself and the people who did not have the courage to do what was right. To be the very best person you can be. Just like the story and in the movie *The Wizard of Oz*, you find happiness in your own backyard.

Genus of What is to Follow

Beep, beep, yeah. Yes, we had been there, but as they say, "Be careful for what you wish for because you just might get it." I am the worst one to be giving such advice, but I understand how we go into such a mess and how we are taken in into making so many purchases. How come we are being chased and howled every day and still need more? I guess it's all due to the greed, and I am able to get it. Good or bad, that's just the facts as I see it. What's going on? Maybe it's time to question yourself (once again) what it is you want and at what cost. All this is an ongoing story as you find out how you are and what good you can do and what really makes you happy.

Growing Trends

The rumor is true; George Lucas is converting the *Star Wars* saga to 3-D. It was over thirty years ago; Lucas spun a tale a long, long time ago in a galaxy far, far away. Lucasfilms has announced plans to redo all six *Star Wars* installments into 3-D and release it into theaters. The first entry will be *Episode 1: The Phantom Menace* in 2012. The films will be distributed by 20th Century Fox.

As you know, 3-D TV, Blu-ray player, glass, and 3-D movies are already for sale. Be sure and don't be surprised if you see this new format in your living room in less than five years. These are just my views. There will be a big sales push to see this happen as more films hit the big screen. There are a few things to work out, of course, but I'm sure you and your family will be entertained and give you a new experience to enjoy.

E-books: Will It Get Kids to Read?

"A study, conducted by Education and Media Company Scholastic and Harrison Group, a marketing and research consultant. Parents are concern the greater the access to technology would limit time reading or with family. 40 percent believe time spent on line, or mobile devices would reduce time for books. Thirty-three percent feats the technology would lead to less time with the family."

The study showed that technology encouraged kids to read. The study also showed parents and kids have strong s on what read is. Text message was also part of the study.

Apple May Unveil Next iPad, June 2011

More than three billion iPads were sold in the tablet debut; they may introduce a new version in the second quarter of 2011. The creation of a smaller seven-inch version of the iPad hasn't finalized a mini-USB drive and built-in camera. Last quarter, iPads accounted for $217 billion (United States) or 12 percent of Apple's overall sales, more than the nine-year-old iPod. The iPad went on sale in April 2010.

Price War as RIM and HP Chase iPad

Apple is leading in the tablet computer. RIM and HP, Acer Inc., LG Electronics Inc., Samsung Electronics, and Dell Inc. are quick to join the race. Apple used the iPod to build a market for a device that packed more features than a smartphone yet is more compact than a laptop. "A price war is inevitable!" RIM, it said, may change as little as $299 (United States) with a two-year contract with AT&T Inc. Investors will stay attuned to whether competition leads to narrowing margins. It is said that Apple's sales could top 50 million next year, with Apple taking a majority of them.

Nintendo slashes profit forecast as investors panic and game is delayed.

As stated in the Toronto newspaper:

> CHIBA. JAPAN—Nintendo slashed its earnings forecast by more than half Wednesday after announcing that its 3DS games machine, packed with glasses-free 3-D technology, won't be ready to go on sale for Christmas.

The article ended by saying,

> Nintendo is likely taking time to perfect the technology, as well as giving more time for outside software developers to come up with games. The next day, investors reacted, causing Nintendo shares to drop!

So it goes, which got to my point—if you're in these technology games, you better bone up on your education.

Here now is the 2010 fall edition of *Mac/Life iPhone Handbook*:

44 Killer iPhone Apps reviewed
Power Tips for IOS
IPhones cases, ear buds, ducks, chargers, and more—Tested
HOW THE IPHONE CAN SUPERCHARGE YOUR ENTIRE
     DAY
40 TIPS IN 24 HOURS
AMAZING ADD-ONS
Pilot a helicopter with your iPhone?
1 YES!
CD INSIDE!
150 free ringtones / 4 how to do videos and more!

You may as well say, "But I cannot afford any of this," and further your education course.

There are many good libraries, free workshops, all kinds of weekend shows featuring many workshops and lectures. For me, my expense is over-the-top. There are many shows I want to attend, but money is tight. My feelings are always the same, I am reassured of what I am crazy about, is still very much alive.

What else can I do? There are a lot of free fitness classes that I am taking, one is a course called Gentle Fitness three times a week. It is free, and it's for people over fifty years old. Get involved with the community, do volunteer your talents. Been there, still do that.

Take some cooking classes, read newspapers and magazines more.

Further Information

Advertising Culture in Canada Through the Baby Boomer Decades

You have seen my account of the times I lived through, of the entire world events, and how it affected me and many. Now we will see how advertising affected Canada through each of these decades.

Canada always had its own distinct voice, the voice of CBC Voice of Doom with Lorne Greene. *Hockey Night in Canada* began airing on Saturday nights on CBC television in 1952; once, just weeks after television broadcasting commenced in Canada, it retained Esso as sponsor. It continued to feature regular season NHL games on the English network every Saturday evening during the NHL season and retained many of the features such as the Hot Stove Lounge and the three stars selection, which originated as an Imperial Oil gasoline promotion and survived even as sponsorship. It eventually passed from Imperial to Molson and, later, Labatt. Another Canadian TV show, which was uniquely Canadian, was *Front Page Challenge. Front Page Challenge,* television's longest continuously running panel show, was one of the most familiar landmarks on the Canadian broadcasting landscape. During much of its thirty-eight-season run on the Canadian Broadcasting Corporation (CBC), from 1957-95, it was among Canadian television's most popular programs, regularly drawing average audiences of one to two million in the small Canadian market; toward the end, viewership dropped, numbering about five hundred thousand in the show's final season. Sometimes, commercials would capture the essence and imagination of a nation, with Molson's rant, "I AM CANADIAN."

Here are some of the most important news events that happened in Canada. In Canada, through the 1950s to 1950, postwar Canada witnessed the rise in birthrate, coupled with a booming economy. This brought on such things as credit cards and the rapid development of new technology, leading to a new cultural reality. Consumers now had purchase power. Urban development was rapid. Car sales skyrocketed, all in keeping with the commute into the city.

1960-1969

In advertising in 1960s, we see a shift in values, a feeling that was not expressed. Bright colors and radical designs were used too to express the voice of the baby boom generation, which now had buying power. Families were different than the 1960s. Families were spending more time in front of the TV, eating TV dinners. Even though the women's moment was at its beginning, many ads were sexist in content. Men were the breadwinners, and women were the busy homemakers who needed their help and support. In Canada, Pierre Elliott Trudeau was coming into office as justice minister. Canadian identity when Montreal hosted Expo 67 in celebration of the Confederation.

Here are the event highlights in Canada in the 1960s: Bill of Rights was passed, formation of CTV, CCF became NDP (New Denominate Party), invention of the audio cassette, reflection of Diefenbaker. In 1963, the *Canadian Code of Advertising Standards* was published. Lester B. Pearson became prime minister. In 1965, a new Canadian flag was created, CBC TV broadcasted in color; in 1967, the Royal Commission on the Status of Women. Pierre Elliott Trudeau was elected prime minister in 1968, and IMAX movie system was invented.

1970-1979

Popular culture of the early 1970s was greatly influenced by the event of the 1960s with the hippie moment, later on the decade with disco. The trends were influenced, and advertising images focused on the new generation. Slangs like "Coca-Cola: it's the real thing" and Pepsi with "Pepsi Generation." As more women joined the workforce, women gained more buying power. An increase in advertising was clearly seen. The change in the portal of men and women began to emerge. Women were seen now and targeted as independent decision makers in their ads.

1980-1989

The 1980s was viewed as a decade of excess and decadence. Post baby boomers were dubbed Generation X, self-centered and disillusioned with society. Maybe so, but I thought it was a great decade to live through. Canadian culture was beginning to mature and be seen; film, music, and writing had gained international recognition. For me, it got a good start with a lot of rock-and-roll groups and some movies, such as *Goin' Down the Road* and *I Can Hear the Mermaid Sing*. We had the talent; it's just time for the world to notice.

Events in Canada That Shouted Out

The Terry Fox's Marathon of Hope, Canadian space arm contributed to the space rise; Trivial Pursuit was invented and became an international fad. In 1984, Marc Garneau became Canada's first astronaut; in 1986, the Canadian dollar sank to 70 cents against the U.S. dollar. By 1989, the North American free trade agreement was signed with the United States.

1990–1999

With the rise in youth, Generation Y was being recognized as a key to Canadian society, more self-assured and confident than its predecessor. Generation Y now became the new target of advertisers; magazines and specialty stores began to cater to tweens and teens. Advertising scrambled to understand what appealed to this new sophisticated group of young people; surveys and analyses were given. Ads were targeted at Generation Y and were taking interest in their offsprings. More than ever, women were recognized as a key group, and advertisers for products, such as cars, began to target females. Gender and diversity and setting the advertising standards Canada in 1994 was in an effort to promote equality in media. The music and "Hollywood North" boomed. Along with media, the Internet became an integrated part of the Canadian household. Canada now entered the twenty-first century as a growing and prosperous nation.

The Event in Canada

The creation of the World Wide Web Internet and Goods and Services Tax (GST)

Kim Campbell became the first female prime minister in 1995; Ebay was formed. In 1998, *Titanic* was directed by Canada's own James Cameron; Adrienne Clarkson became governor-general.

2000–2009: The Decade to Watch Out For

This is the decade of fear, terrorism, superbugs, mad cow, financial meltdown, global warming, and so on. We began with the scare of Y2K, and we are ending it with Copenhagen.

As we look back on the decade, it is useful to zero in on some of the big events and major changes that have shaken up Canada.

1. September 11, 2001—The attacks on 9/11 have had the same effect. Little did we know that this would lead to Canada going to war with Afghanistan in 2002, and the war still builds on.

2. The sponsorship scandal—When Auditor General Sheila Fraser revealed in 2004 that the Chrétien government's sponsorship program in Quebec was rife with corruption, Canada lost its last little bit of innocence. Have a nice day.

3. The BlackBerry—People never check e-mails and surf the Net while driving when the decade began like they do now. The Blackberry (and later the iPhone and their equivalents) have made the Web mobile, your very own office in your pocket or purse.

4. The resurrection of the Tories—After the Progressive Conservative Party went from a majority to just two seats in the 1993 federal election, it looked like the Tories would never recover. A Unite the Right movement brought the Canadian Alliance party (formerly the Reform Party) and the old Progressive Conservative Party together in 2003. Things still looked pretty shaky, but their new leader Stephen Harper managed to hold it together, win the 2006 election, and stay in power for the rest of the decade.

5. China—From the Beijing Olympics to tainted toys, China loomed large in the minds of Canadians in ways it never did before. We now had to watch out what kids played with. China, moreover, was short-term for India and other latent economic powers that are changing the global economic game. It remains to be seen how Canada will perform in this new environment.

6. The dot-com bubble bursts—At the dawn of the decade, everyone wanted to work for a dot-com company. Many of those who did had pink slips by 2001. Generation X finally thought things were going its way only to wind up roughly where it was when it came of age in the recession of the early 1990s. The tech sector survived, but only after $5 trillion in the market value of technology companies was wiped out from March 2000 to October 2002. This was not the get rich quick it claimed to be.

7. Al Gore stars in a movie—*An Inconvenient Truth* premiered in 2006 and set off a huge wave of concern about global warming. The Intergovernmental Panel on Climate Change dates back to 1988, and the Kyoto Protocol goes back to 1997, but arguably, it was Gore's slideshow that really got the ball rolling in terms of public interest in the issue. It was the big dissolution at the table all weekend.

8. $50 oil—Don't you mean $150 oil? Nope. Oil was dirt cheap throughout the 1990s, and when the new decade started, it was

under $30 a barrel. As we got deeper into the 2000s, Canada West Foundation's chief economist was called an idiot when he said that oil might hit $50 a barrel, which of course it did. But it wasn't until 2008 that oil prices went nuts, and anyone who told you that they know what will happen in the next decade had a bridge to sell you. This was a bad time to have a car.

9. The great recession—Recessions come and go, but maybe because this one is still upon us, it seems different. This is my second recession; every time it is announced, that is when it kicks in. For one, we know that it was more than just a natural downturn of the business.

10. Gay culture goes mainstream—Liberty and the celebration, it's both good and bad. It also forces standards on everyone else. They have the right; now it's okay. But the fight for true equally still builds on.

This is the end, my friend, my friend, my friend. For now, you can see how I, a baby boomer, lived his life through many troubled times, always doing exactly what I wanted. Now in these deeds, all is almost forgotten. Be careful, old or young, because you may get whatever you're after. I hope you were entertained, inspired, and given something to think about. It's a wonderful life and far from over. There are exciting new things to come; we have all new things to learn, a lot of old habits to get rid of. The best thing you can do for now is get back in and believe in yourself. Just don't spend all your money!

The End

Baby Boom, Boom will return

Baby Boom, Boom—as seen on TV

Information came from the following books:

Out of the Garden: Toys and Children's Culture in the Age of TV Marketing
    by Stephan Kline
ISBN 0-9200059-65-1 Garamond Press

Encyclopedia of Culture by Jane and Michael Stern
ISBN 0-06-096972-5 Harper Perennial

James Bond in the Cinema by John Brosnan
ISBN 0-900-73047-1 A.S. Barnes and Co., Inc. Printed in UK

Mac/Life presents *iPhone: Handbook*
Fall 2010, Future US, Inc.

Advertising: Reflections of Culture and Values by Rose Fine-Meyer and
    Stephanie K. Gibson ISBN 0-921156-73-1 Rubicon publisher

Further reading list:

Chips & Pop: Decoding the Nexus Generation by Robert Barnard, Dave
    Cosgrave, and Jennifer Welsh
ISBN 1-89421-08-2 Malcolm Lester Books

Saturday Morning TV: Thirty Years of the Shows You Waited All Week to Watch
    by Gary Grossman
ISBN 0-440-58361-6 Dell Publishing

Ready Steady, Go!: The Smashing Rise and Giddy Fall of Swinging London
    by Shawn Levy
ISBN 0-385-4957-8 published by Doubleday

National Geographic: The Ultimate Field Guide to Photography by Bob Martin,
    Richard Olsenius, Robert Clark, John Healy, and Debbi Grossman
ISBN 977-14262-0105-5

INDEX

Let me hear your questions, your story's about, you and your cousins, and how your going to make your life better.

bean_bond@rogers.com